WOMEN WIN
THE VOTE

Turning Points IN·AMERICAN·HISTORY

WOMEN WIN THE VOTE

Betsy Covington Smith

Silver Burdett Press, Inc.
Englewood Cliffs, New Jersey

Acknowledgments

The author thanks the following individuals and institutions for their assistance in the creation of this book: Karen E. Bedford, the League of Women Voters; Josephine Weathers, Madame Walker Urban Life Center, Inc.; Margaret Hilles Meiklejohn, the daughter of Elizabeth McShane Hilles; Jacqueline Ogburn; The Seneca Falls Historical Society; and Judy Hart, Women's Rights National Historical Park.

Consultants:

We thank the following people for reviewing the manuscript and offering their helpful suggestions:

Elizabeth Blackmar
Assistant Professor of History
Columbia College, New York

Gloria Contreras
Professor
College of Education
North Texas State University

Cover, title page, and contents page illustrations courtesy of the Library of Congress.

Library of Congress Cataloging-in-Publication Data

Smith, Betsy Covington.
    Women win the vote / by Betsy Covington Smith.
        p.   cm.—(Turning points in American history)
    Bibliography: p.
    Includes index.
    Summary: Details the history of women in America from 1620 to the present as they have fought for freedom, equality, and particularly the right to vote.
    1. Women—Suffrage—United States—History—Juvenile literature.
[1. Women—Suffrage. 2. Women's rights.] I. Title. II. Series.
JK1898.S65   1989
324.6′23′0973—dc20
    ISBN 0-382-09854-4 (pbk.) ISBN 0-382-09837-4 (lib. bdg.)

Editorial coordination by Richard G. Gallin

 Created by Media Projects Incorporated

C. Carter Smith, *Executive Editor*
Toni Rachiele, *Managing Editor*
Charles Wills, *Project Editor*
Bernard Schleifer, *Design Consultant*
Simon Hu, *Cartographer*

ISBN 0-382-09837-4 [lib. bdg.]
10 9 8 7 6 5 4 3 2 1

ISBN 0-382-09854-4 [pbk.]
10 9 8 7 6 5 4 3 2 1

CONTENTS

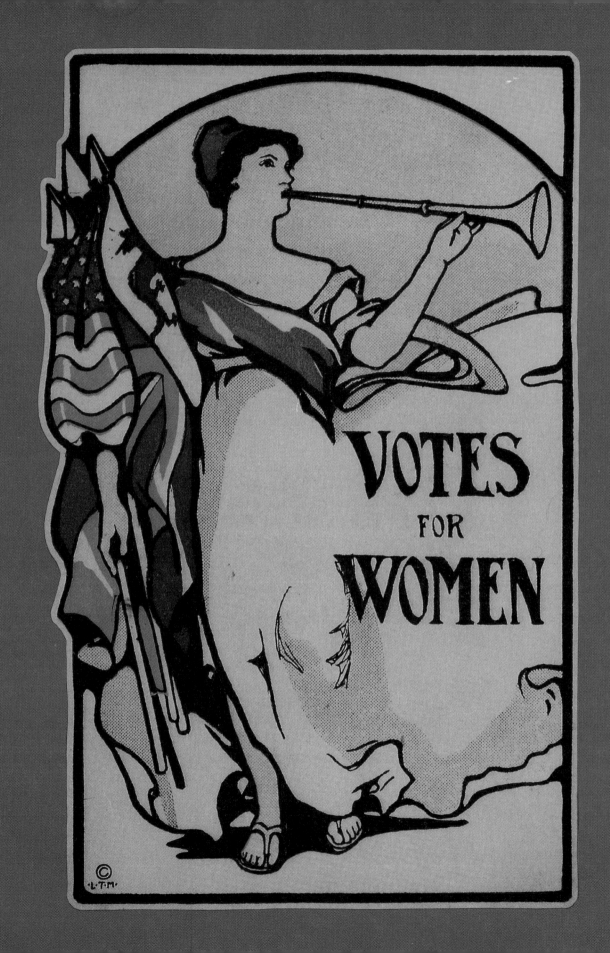

INTRODUCTION

I AM IN CELL 30, SECOND TIER . . .

Friday, November 16, 1917

I am in cell 30, second tier . . .

So begins the prison diary of Elizabeth McShane. Her crime? She simply wanted to vote.

As a member of Alice Paul's Woman's Party, Elizabeth had been among a group of women picketing the White House on behalf of woman's suffrage—the right to vote. At the same time, inside the White House, President Woodrow Wilson had been meeting with the French ambassador. Embarrassed by the constant sight of the silent protesters, President Wilson had had the entire group arrested and put in jail.

The prisoners included many important women, wives of well-known men. Together they asked prison authorities to treat them as "political prisoners." They asked to be allowed to wear their

A pro-suffrage poster from the early twentieth century.

own clothes, exercise, and receive mail and food from the outside. All requests were denied.

Elizabeth McShane's notes, scribbled from behind bars, continue:

My mind feels much confused. I wonder if we have come in vain. I am with Mrs. Harvey Wiley, wife of the Chief of the U.S. Public Health Service.

Saturday, November 17, 1917

I have declared hunger-strike to Mrs. Waters, the matron. Others, except Mrs. Wiley and I, have boiled cabbage, boiled ham, bread and tea.

Wednesday, November 21

Mr. Zinkham, the prison warden, said he wishes to Heaven the Commissioner would let him treat us as political prisoners. Lucy Burns has been fed forcibly twice in a most cruel way, hurting her lips and face.

Friday, November 23

This is the most despairing moment of my

Members of Alice Paul's Woman's Party picket the White House. Many were jailed for their vocal demand for a federal suffrage amendment.

life. Every instinct within me has been outraged, hurt, and insulted, for I have been forcibly fed. Dr. Ladd came with a tube that looked like a hose and a pint of eggs and milk. He rammed it down so fast that I couldn't breathe. Then he poured food in rapidly. I gagged and the food came up as fast as it went down. It is so degrading! I told Dr. Ladd that I had been brought up as a lady, not a pig, and that I might have taken a small quantity slowly, but not a pint at a gulp. He said nothing.

Monday, November 26

That awful tube has been rammed down my throat again. I've drunk a quart of strong mustard water, but my stomach clings to that food as to a long-lost brother. I'm so

humiliated, but dare not take ipecac [a medicine that causes vomiting] on top of mustard. Edith's cheering letter has just come. I love these letters, but they make me feel so small and far away and the prison bars so strong.

When Elizabeth McShane was eighty years old, in 1971, she gave to her daughters the prison diary she'd written more than fifty years earlier. With it was a note, saying, "I don't remember how many times I went to jail, but these seem to be the only times I made notes." And she added, "I was lucky to be in jail [again] at the end of the campaign. I remember when the word came that Pres. Wilson had called Congress into special session to pass the suffrage amendment—the 19th—'The right of citizens of the United States to vote shall not be denied or abridged by the United States or by any State on account of sex.'"

Before joining the battle for the right of women to vote, Elizabeth McShane had graduated from Vassar College with a Phi Beta Kappa key, the highest academic honor a student can achieve. After her release from prison, she helped teach medical students at Massachusetts General Hospital about industrial diseases. She married in 1924, raised a family, and taught high school for twenty-five years in Massachusetts, Rhode Island, and Pennsylvania. Yet, of all her accomplishments, the one she prized the most was the commitment and sacrifice she had made for the cause of woman's suffrage.

In fighting for the right to vote, Elizabeth McShane was only a foot soldier in the final stages of a battle that had lasted seventy-five years, testing the courage and stamina of thousands of women. It was a battle that had to be fought. For as even the earliest suffrage leaders had realized, women could never hope to shed their inferior status in society or win further rights without the vote. Indeed, the vote was the one thing that would make them, finally, full citizens of their country.

In 1915 a motorcade carried the "Woman's Liberty Bell" from California to Washington. Elizabeth McShane is in the front seat.

1

THE ROAD TO SENECA FALLS

American women won the vote in a battle against prejudice that spanned 300 years. It took that long for women to prove that they possessed enough intelligence and judgment to be full voting citizens in their own country. But from the very beginning women have been an important part of the building of America.

The London merchants who were the founders of the Virginia colony realized that women were needed to build permanent communities in the new world. So, in 1619, 90 "agreeable persons . . . [were] sold with their own consent to settlers as wives." A year later 29 women were among the 101 passengers on the *Mayflower*.

Life was grim for these women. The young Virginia brides had to fight

Pilgrim families walking to church. Women played a vital role in planting permanent settlements in what would become the United States.

against plague and against resistance from Native Americans. In Massachusetts, bitterly cold weather, illness, and hunger left only four of the 29 *Mayflower* women alive after the first winter. At first, simply staying alive was the common goal. While constantly on the alert for attacks from the natives, the colonists worked round the clock. They cleared the land, built their homes, made clothing for their children, and hunted for food. But settling the colonies was too much for them alone. Also, the London merchants wanted to profit from their colonial ventures. Soon, ships came with two completely different types of human cargo: indentured servants and black slaves.

Many indentured servants came to America to escape lives of poverty in England. Others were kidnaped and dragged onto ships bound for America, or were released from overcrowded English prisons. Once here, they became

A COPPIE OF THE LIBERTIES OF THE MASSACHUSETS COLONIE IN NEW ENGLAND.

The free fruition of such liberties Immunities and priveledges as humanitie, Civilitie, and Christianitie call for as due to every man in his place and proportion without impeachment and Infringement hath ever bene and ever will be the tranquillitie and Stabilitie of Churches and Commonwealths. And the deniall or deprivall thereof, the disturbance if not the ruine of both.

We hould it therefore our dutie and safetie whilst we are about the further establishing of this Government to collect and expresse all such freedomes as for present we foresee may concerne us, and our posteritie after us, And to ratify them with our sollemne consent.

We doe therefore this day religiously and unanimously decree and confirme these following Rites, liberties and priveledges concerning our Churches, and Civill State to be respectively impartiallie and inviolably enjoyed and observed throughout our Jurisdiction for ever.

1   No mans life shall be taken away, no mans honour or good name shall be stayned, no mans person shall be arested, restrayned, banished, dismembred, nor any wayes punished, no man shall be deprived of his wife or children, no mans goods or estaite shall be taken away from him, nor any way indammaged under coulor of law or Countenance of Authoritie, unlesse it be by vertue or equitie of some expresse law of the Country waranting the same, established by a generall Court and sufficiently published, or in case of the defect of a law in any perteculer case by the word of god. And in Capitall cases, or in cases concerning dismembring or banishment, according to that word to be judged by the Generall Court.   pag. 1.

2   Every person within this Jurisdiction, whether Inhabitant or forreiner shall enjoy the same justice and law, that is generall for the plantation, which we constitute and execute one towards another without partialitie or delay.   pag. 143.

3   No man shall be urged to take any oath or subscribe any articles, covenants or remonstrance, of a publique and Civill nature, but such as the Generall Court hath considered, allowed, and required.   pag. 219

4   No man shall be punished for not appearing at or before any Civill Assembly, Court, Councell, Magistrate, or Officer, nor for the omission of any office or service, if he shall be necessarily hindred by any apparent Act or providence of God, which he could neither foresee nor avoid. Provided that this law shall not prejudice any person of his just cost or damage, in any civill action.   pag. 4.

5   No man shall be compelled to any publique worke or service unlesse the presse be grounded upon some act of the generall Court, and have reasonable allowance therefore.   pag. 73. sect. 2.
    6. No man

The Massachusetts Body of Liberties, a forerunner of the U.S. Constitution's Bill of Rights. It gives certain rights to men, but says nothing about women's rights.

unpaid servants, bonded to a master for a period of service that lasted from five to seven years, the time it took to work off the cost of their passage. While in service, a bondsman or bondswoman was not allowed to marry or to do other work without the master's consent.

As miserable as the life of a bonded servant could be, there was always the promise of eventual freedom. There was no such hope for the black slave. Slaves were brought from Africa against their will, and were considered mere property. They could be bought, sold, and worked like animals for their whole lives.

With this pool of labor, the colonies grew and flourished, and the resulting prosperity created new social divisions. In the beginning, all women, rich and poor, had worked together with the goal of survival. Now, distinctions in social status separated them, creating many different kinds of "colonial women." A colonial woman could have been a slave in North Carolina, or the mistress of a Virginia tobacco plantation, or an unpaid servant girl, working for a family in New York. Or she might have been a poor farmer's wife, living in the remote hills of western Connecticut, barely able to feed her eight children.

They had one thing in common, however. They lived in America when women had few legal and economic rights. Slave women, of course, had no rights. Married white women were also relatively powerless, since the law regarded them as their husbands' dependents. They could not sign legal contracts and they could not own property. In rare cases of divorce from their husbands, they were not even allowed to keep their own children.

Few colonists, male or female, had any real voice in major issues. These were decided for them by England. Thus, the right to vote, called suffrage, was not a matter of concern until after the Revolutionary War. The only people allowed to vote during the colonial period were property-owning men.

Next to English common law, religion was the most powerful force in determining how women lived. "Thy desire shall be to thy husband and he shall rule over thee," said the Bible, and colonial women obeyed. Religion taught that women were inferior to men, fit only for marriage and motherhood. At the same time, idleness was considered a sin. So white colonial women were expected to sew, weave, make soap, shoes, and candles, and do all the other work of caring for their families.

There were other American women whose lives were untouched by colonial rules of behavior: the Native Americans. Although some tribes viewed women as nothing more than childbearers and workers, other tribes gave their women enormous power. All inheritance in the Delaware tribe, for instance, came down through the female line. In the Seneca tribe, the old women who served as clan mothers appointed the male tribal chiefs.

The colonists, too, gave women more power when the times demanded it. In the early colonial period, men and women were much closer to being equal. Then, no one worried about whether a man or woman was doing a particular job, as long as that job was done. After the Revolutionary War, as people migrated west, the same thing happened. Pioneer women learned to do anything necessary to keep their families alive, including hunting and trapping.

Colonial life was hard. Children lost fathers, and wives buried husbands. Often, widows continued their husband's businesses. Other widows became seamstresses or servants to support themselves and their children. All of this happened at a time when women were looked upon as unsuitable for most kinds of work. But from the earliest colonial days, the image of the strong pioneer woman helped undermine the notion of women's inferiority.

The first person to publicly question the role of women in colonial America was Anne Hutchinson, who came to Boston in 1634. The Puritans who ruled the Massachusetts Bay Colony believed that only a few men could speak for

Barred from churches by the Puritan government, Anne Hutchinson preaches in her Boston house.

God since they, alone, were God's "chosen." Rebelling against this idea, the deeply religious Anne Hutchinson began preaching in her home. Because she was a woman, she had received no formal education, but she knew the Bible and was a fine speaker. She criticized local ministers and expressed her belief that all people were equal before God.

To defy religion in Puritan Boston was unthinkable, for the church was the government. To maintain that all were equal in God's sight was to claim that she and everyone else were the equals of the men who ruled Massachusetts. Governor John Winthrop and his associates moved quickly to suppress this

According to a popular story, "Molly Pitcher" took command of her husband's cannon after he was wounded in the Battle of Monmouth in 1778.

LIBRARY OF CONGRESS

dangerous idea. They attacked Hutchinson through a court trial and religious proceedings. As a woman, she stood no chance. She was exiled from the colony.

Shortly after Hutchinson's trouble in Massachusetts, Margaret Brent challenged the status quo in Maryland. Brent had settled there in 1638. Because of her well-connected family in England, she had been given large land grants, which made her the first woman in Maryland to own land. After she helped Governor Leonard Calvert suppress a rebellion by assembling armed volunteers, he appointed her legal manager of his estate. The Provincial Court was impressed by her abilities and appointed her attorney for Lord Baltimore. As manager of both estates, Margaret Brent entered more lawsuits than anyone else in Maryland. She decided to appeal to Maryland's House of Burgesses for not one but *two* votes, since she was Lord Baltimore's attorney and a large landowner herself. Shocked that a woman could be so bold, the governor denied her request. Margaret Brent moved to Virginia rather than submit to the decision.

For more than a hundred years after Anne Hutchinson and Margaret Brent, the status of women remained unchanged. But wartimes have always been times of change in the roles and rights of women. The Revolutionary War was no exception. Because many men were serving in the Continental armies, women had to step into their jobs at home. Perhaps the major contribution women made to the Revolutionary

War effort was supplying clothes and food to the army. Under the direction of Esther DeBerdt Reed, wife of George Washington's adjutant general, thousands of women raised enough money to buy the cloth needed to make shirts for their fighting men. This was the first recorded instance of American women organizing to work toward a specific goal, an essential ability for later fights for woman's rights.

After the war, American life could not remain the same. Explosive ideas were in the air: freedom, independence, equality. If men were endowed with certain "inalienable rights," what about women? If government was to be run with the "consent of the governed," then why were women not allowed to have a voice in that consent? One state—New Jersey—did allow women to vote on local affairs in the 1780s. But for the most part, the status of women in America was unchanged by the Revolutionary War.

In 1776 Abigail Adams, wife of the revolutionary leader and future president John Adams, wrote to her husband:

> In the new code of laws . . . I desire you remember the ladies and be more generous and favorable to them than your ancestors. Do not put such unlimited power into the hands of the husbands. Remember, all men would be tyrants if they could. If particular care and attention is not paid to the ladies, we are determined to foment a rebellion, and will not hold ourselves bound by any laws in which we have no representation.

GILBERT STUART, NATIONAL GALLERY OF ART, GIFT OF MRS. ROBERT HOMANS.

Abigail Adams, wife of a future president, urged her husband to be "more generous and favorable" to women in making laws for the new United States.

Although Abigail Adams was writing privately, she was as far ahead of her time in expressing these ideas as Margaret Brent had been ahead of hers.

The first important issue in the long struggle for woman's rights was higher education for women. The idea was first publicly expressed by Judith Sargeant Murray, daughter of a Massachusetts merchant. She wrote an essay, published in 1790, pointing out the lack of educational opportunities for women:

> Will it be said that the judgment of a male two years old is more sage than that of a female's of the same age? . . . But from that period on what partiality! How is the one exalted and the other depressed, by the contrary modes of education that are adopted!

The one is taught to aspire, the other is early confined and limited. As their years increase, the sister must be wholly domesticated, while the brother is led by hand through all the flowery paths of science.

But despite the pleas of Judith Murray and a few others, higher education for women made little progress. Girls from prosperous families learned to play the harpsichord and embroider. Most girls learned the skills of housewifery.

But great changes were happening throughout the young nation. In 1814 the first power-driven looms appeared in Massachusetts and were operated by women. At about the same time, much of the West was opened for settlement. Suddenly, teachers were needed for the growing population. With women already working in the mills, it became difficult to maintain that teaching was not a job for women. Furthermore, female teachers could be paid less than men. But first someone had to teach the teachers.

Emma Hart Willard was a major leader in education for women. As a child, she had been given a broad education by her father. She realized, after teaching for several years, that what women needed was a formal course of study. With help from the citizens of Troy, New York, she opened the Troy Female Seminary in 1821. It was the first high school devoted solely to the education of girls. Even though her school was private, she made sure that no one was prevented from enrolling for lack of funds. Often she lent the girls the money, asking to be paid back only after her pupils had found teaching jobs.

The first institution to offer an academic course to women comparable to that of men at the college level was Oberlin College in Ohio, which was founded in 1833. The college declared itself open to anyone, regardless of race or sex. Among the first Oberlin graduates were Lucy Stone, who became one of the outstanding orators of the early woman's rights movement, and Antoinette Brown, the first ordained woman minister in the nation. In those days, however, Oberlin believed its role was to prepare women for futures as wives and mothers.

By the 1840s Northern women were on the move. Thousands were working in the mills of New England, teaching school, and settling the West. Most important, both black and white women became active in one of the leading social causes of the day: abolitionism, the fight to end slavery.

In the 1830s there had been a great outcry against slavery. After Nat Turner, a slave, had led a revolt in Virginia in 1831, slave owners throughout the South had adopted tougher measures to control the slaves. That same year in Boston the abolitionist William Lloyd Garrison had founded a weekly newspaper, *The Liberator*, devoted to the fight against slavery.

Since Anne Hutchinson's time, it had been considered improper for women to speak out publicly. One of the earliest women to break through this curtain of

Slaves dance in this nineteenth-century painting. Women played a major role in the abolitionist movement, which sought to free the slaves.

silence was a black woman, Maria W. Stewart. She was uneducated, strongly religious, and an outspoken abolitionist. She gave several speeches in Boston from 1831 and 1833, pleading not only for the slave but also for her right as a woman to speak in public.

In 1833 the American Anti-Slavery Society was founded in Philadelphia. Women could not join the society, but they were allowed to attend and to address the convention, and when the convention ended, a group of women formed the Philadelphia Female Anti-Slavery Society. Soon women in every major northeastern city had formed similar societies. In 1837 the first National Female Anti-Slavery Society met in New York, with 81 delegates from 12 states attending.

Most of the women who became leaders in the suffrage movement were actively involved in the abolitionist movement. They learned how to organize on a large scale. They learned political methods such as going door-to-door to get people to sign antislavery petitions. And perhaps most important, they broke the taboo that prohibited women from speaking out publicly for what they believed.

Two of the most effective speakers against slavery were Sarah and Angelina Grimké, two sisters from South Carolina. They were raised in a slave-owning family but grew to hate slavery.

After moving to Philadelphia, Angelina wrote an essay urging white Southern women to fight against the practice. Both sisters were then invited to speak in New York.

Their first lecture was well attended: more than 300 women came to listen to the sisters' eloquent, firsthand account of the evils of slavery. Their reputation grew. Before long they were speaking before huge audiences of men and women throughout the North. Since public speaking was not considered proper behavior for nineteenth-century white women, they were attacked from all sides. Had they been men, they realized, there would have been no criticism. From then on, they began linking the issue of slavery with the low position of women. In so doing, they forced the women in their audiences to consider the injustices in their own lives.

Women were organizing on other fronts. The "mill girls" of New England had begun their battle for better wages and working conditions. During the first half of the nineteenth century, women worked in more than a hundred industrial occupations. Many worked at home, bent over their sewing machines for 13 or 14 hours a day. The average home worker's pay was $1.25 or less a week, compared with the $6 a week that the lowest-paid male workers could earn. Conditions in the factories were only slightly better. The working day ran from 12 to 16 hours. Most of the women were teenage girls who made from $1 to $3 weekly. Out of their wages, the women had to pay $1.50 to $1.75 to live in company-owned boardinghouses where as many as six women lived in the same small room.

The earliest known strike by women workers took place in Pawtucket, Rhode Island, in 1824. They joined striking men to protest a wage cut and longer hours. This was followed by an all-woman strike in 1828 in Dover, New Hampshire. Throughout the 1830s and 1840s women in hundreds of New England towns went on strikes, protest marches, and walkouts that sometimes resulted in temporary gains but did not permanently improve their situation.

In December 1844 five "mill girls" in Lowell, Massachusetts, met to plan how to win a ten-hour working day. What was needed, they decided, was *organization*, similar to the antislavery campaign. They formed the Lowell Female Labor Reform Association, taking as their motto the phrase "Try again." By May 1845 they had 600 members and a president, Sarah Bagley. A tireless advocate for the cause, Sarah Bagley wrote articles, gave speeches, and organized Female Labor Reform groups in other towns.

The Lowell Female Labor Reform Association launched a petition campaign asking the Massachusetts Legislature for a ten-hour day. Swamped by the huge number of petitions the women had collected, the lawmakers were forced to hold hearings. To the surprise of all, Bagley and her associates were not at all afraid of testifying before the leaders of the state. Calmly and forcefully, they described the unhealthful

Though many nineteenth-century women worked in mills and factories, they were almost always paid less than men. Here, women shoemakers in Lynn, Massachusetts, march in protest.

work conditions. Unfortunately, the lawmakers sided with the mill owners. But Sarah Bagley got even. She and the other women mounted a successful campaign to defeat the chairman of the hearings in his bid for reelection.

These early labor movement women did not succeed in building their own labor organization. But they did prove that they knew how to organize, how to develop leadership with ability and courage, and how to build a stable organization. The petition campaign demonstrated that they could use political action techniques effectively in the fight to better their own lives.

The stage was set. Through education, abolition, and labor reform, women gained the tools to wage their own struggle to become full American citizens. There was now a network of women who knew each other, who knew how to organize, and who had new ideas about what women could do.

The time was right for the first woman's rights convention, to be held in Seneca Falls, New York, in 1848. But as early leader Lucretia Mott wondered, would anyone bother to come?

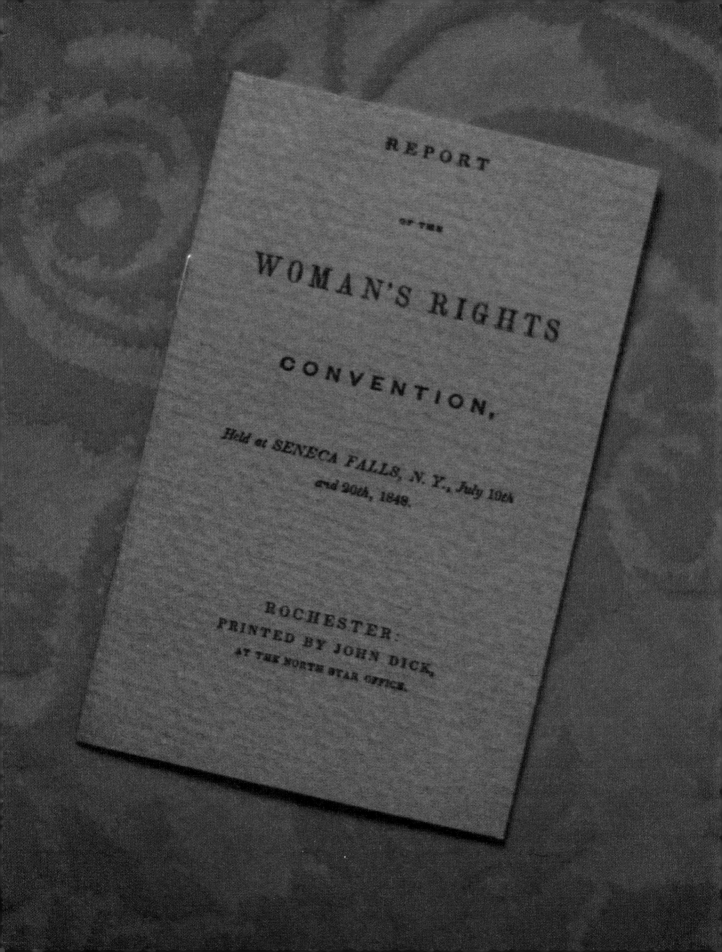

REPORT

OF THE

WOMAN'S RIGHTS

CONVENTION,

Held at SENECA FALLS, N. Y., July 19th
and 20th, 1848.

ROCHESTER:
PRINTED BY JOHN DICK,
AT THE NORTH STAR OFFICE.

2

VOICES ARE HEARD

The seeds for the Seneca Falls convention had been planted several years earlier. At the 1840 World Anti-Slavery Convention in London, some of the American delegates were women. At the last minute, the convention ruled that only men could participate. Among those forced to watch from the gallery were Lucretia Coffin Mott and Elizabeth Cady Stanton.

The older of the two, Lucretia Mott, had been born on Nantucket Island, Massachusetts, in 1793. As a Quaker, she had never felt the bonds that restricted other women. A strong tradition of equality existed among Quakers, particularly on Nantucket. She had taught school when she was just a teenager. After marrying James Mott, an abolitionist, she became a Quaker minister and joined her husband in the antislavery cause. A kind, gentle woman

This report was published after the Seneca Falls Convention of 1848, a major milestone on the road to woman's suffrage.

Lucretia Coffin Mott. With Elizabeth Stanton, she planned and led the Seneca Falls Convention.

with principles of steel, she had become a much-loved public figure by the time she came to London.

Elizabeth Cady Stanton was the young wife of abolitionist leader Henry Stanton. She and Mrs. Mott began talking. Both had lively minds and enjoyed discussing ideas. What was the use of

Elizabeth Stanton and her daughter.

women working hard for a cause like abolitionism, they wondered bitterly, if women had no power to change things?

Elizabeth Stanton was born in 1815 in Albany, New York. She had a good mind that had been stimulated by a first-rate education. Stanton had also learned some unforgettable lessons at home. Because her father was a judge, women often came to him for help when their husbands had abandoned them, leaving them without money, property, or even their own children. But there was nothing he could do to help them. Married women had no rights to their own property or children.

After the London convention, Mott and Stanton wrote to each other regularly. In time, Elizabeth and Henry Stanton moved to Seneca Falls, a small town in western New York. With her husband often away from home, Mrs. Stanton felt lonely and trapped. Every day brought the same exhausting routine: cooking, cleaning, washing, sewing, caring for her children.

In early July 1848 Lucretia Mott was visiting her sister in a town near Seneca Falls. Stanton spent the day with her, the sister, and two other women. As she later wrote, "I poured out, that day, the torrent of my accumulating discontent, with such vehemence and indignation that I stirred myself, as well as the rest of the party, to do and dare anything." The five women decided to call a meeting to discuss woman's rights. Stanton went home and put a notice in the Seneca Falls *Courier* of July 14, saying that the meeting would be five days later on July 19 and 20. Then she began planning the meeting.

She started by reading the American Declaration of Independence aloud to herself. She had an idea. What if she were to add the word *women* wherever possible? For instance, "We hold these truths to be self-evident, that all men *and women* are created equal." She drew up a list of demands: woman's rights to own property, to control her own earnings, to share in the custody of her children, to gain an education, and to enter a profession. She realized that some rights required changes in laws, but if women could vote, they could change the laws.

The Stanton House in Seneca Falls, New York, where Elizabeth Stanton planned the first women's rights convention in the United States.

Giving women the right to vote was a shocking idea in 1848. "Thou will make us ridiculous. We must go slowly," warned Lucretia Mott. Elizabeth's husband, Henry Stanton, threatened to leave town if she insisted upon including a resolution on giving women the vote in the meeting's agenda. But Frederick Douglass, the famous black abolitionist, sent a note approving her proposal and promising to speak at the convention. Elizabeth Stanton did not back down. True to his word, Henry Stanton left town.

Even on such short notice, three hundred people came, including at least forty men. They arrived at the little Wesleyan Chapel in Seneca Falls from 50 miles around. Stanton opened the meeting with a brilliant speech, followed with an address by Frederick Douglass. The right of women to vote was Resolution 9, which carried by only a small margin. But in the end sixty-eight women and thirty-two men signed the Declaration of Principles. Among them was nineteen-year-old Charlotte Woodward, who dreamed of becoming a typesetter in a print shop. She was the only one present who lived long enough to vote in a national election.

When the women left Seneca Falls, they had no way of knowing that a movement had been launched that would alter the lives of their daughters and granddaughters. But they knew that their own lives had changed. Never again would they feel quite so alone, for they realized now that there were hundreds, perhaps thousands, of women also rebelling against the conditions in their lives.

The times were ripe for the kinds of ideas introduced at Seneca Falls. The United States was changing rapidly. There were 225,512 women in manufacturing jobs by 1850. Everywhere new ideas were being discussed and old ways discarded. A few women had distinguished themselves. Elizabeth Blackwell, the first woman doctor, graduated from Geneva College in 1849. Dorothea Dix had begun issuing reports about the terrible conditions in prisons and insane asylums. Successful novels were published by Catherine Sedgwick, Fanny Fern, and Harriet Beecher Stowe. Stowe's *Uncle Tom's Cabin*, an abolitionist novel, sold 300,000 copies in one year.

The woman's movement continued to grow. In 1850 the first National Woman's Rights Convention was held in Worcester, Massachusetts. It was denounced by one newspaper as "a motley gathering of fanatical mongrels, male and female, of fugitive slaves and fugitive lunatics." Nonetheless, it drew a thousand people from eleven states and brought together the emerging leaders of the movement for the first

Harriet Beecher Stowe's novel about slavery, Uncle Tom's Cabin, *won many converts for the abolition movement. Staged versions of the book, like the one advertised here, were also very popular.*

time. Of these, no one would prove more valuable to the cause than Lucy Stone.

Born in 1818, Lucy was one of seven children of a farmer who scratched out a living in western Massachusetts. "Oh dear!" cried her mother when Lucy was born. "I am sorry it is a girl. A woman's life is so hard." Lucy Stone began teaching school at sixteen. She saved up enough from her small salary to go to Oberlin College. Upon graduating in 1847, she began a career in public speaking as an abolitionist. "I expect to plead not for the slave alone, but for suffering humanity everywhere. Especially do I mean to labor for the elevation of my sex."

Lucy became a lecturer for the Anti-Slavery Society. Her voice was so clear and musical that it calmed even the angriest of the pro-slavery people in her audiences. Like the Grimké sisters, however, she couldn't keep the subjects of slavery and woman's rights apart. This annoyed the abolitionists who had hired her. So Lucy agreed to lecture against slavery only on weekends, if she could speak about woman's rights the rest of the week.

By the mid–1850s the leaders of the woman's movement were taking their places. Elizabeth Stanton was its most outstanding intellect and philosopher. Lucy Stone was its most brilliant orator. There was only one more skill that was needed: organization. That was the gift of Susan B. Anthony, perhaps the greatest leader of them all.

Susan Anthony was born into a

THE NATIONAL PORTRAIT GALLERY, SMITHSONIAN INSTITUTION

Lucy Stone, who became the leader of the American Woman Suffrage Association.

Quaker family in Adams, Massachusetts, in 1820 and moved to Rochester, New York, as a child. As a young woman she taught school, but she quit in disgust over the practice of paying women teachers much less than men. She became a worker for the temperance movement, battling the liquor industry and saloonkeepers for laws to control the serving of alcohol. Again, Anthony saw the futility of working for a cause when women had no power to reform things. In 1851 she met Stanton and was so impressed that the woman's movement became her life's work.

During the 1850s a national woman's rights convention was held every year except 1857. Voting was not the main issue. In those early years rights such as

Fiery Sojourner Truth, a former slave, fought against slavery and for women's rights.

control of property, opportunities for education, and child custody were more important. Some men were furious that women demanded so much. At a woman's convention in Akron, Ohio, in 1851, a clergyman gave a speech ridiculing the weakness of women. Some men present began laughing and heckling from the audience. Suddenly, a tall, gaunt former slave named Sojourner Truth mounted the podium. Although she had never learned to read or write, she turned the full force of her fury on the man who had been speaking:

> Look at my arm! I have ploughed and planted and gathered into barns and no man could head me—and ain't I a woman? I could work as much and eat as much as a man—when I could get it—and bear the lash as well! And ain't I a woman? I have born thirteen children, and seen most of 'em sold into slavery, and when I cried out with my mother's grief, none but Jesus heard me—and ain't I a woman?

Sojourner Truth had been born in New York state and given the name Isabella. She had been forbidden by her owner to marry the man she loved, but after marriage to a man that her owner had selected, she gained her freedom in 1827 when New York passed a law forbidding slavery in the state. She worked as a domestic servant in New York City, then joined the abolitionist movement, taking the name Sojourner Truth. Like the Grimké sisters and Lucy Stone, Truth convinced many women that they were as capable of bringing about changes in society as men were. Even when faced with ridicule and threats of violence, she fearlessly continued to speak out against slavery and for the rights of women.

Women were also attacked by the newspapers. To exchange ideas and information they had to rely on the abolitionist journals or journals of their own. One of these was *The Lily*, published by Amelia Bloomer in Seneca Falls. It was in this paper that the "bloomer costume" first appeared. It was an attempt to introduce clothing more fitting for active, independent women than the floor-length dresses then in style. For several years, all the leaders of the woman's rights movement wore the "bloomer costume," which consisted of a tunic to the knees, worn over ankle-length Turkish pantaloons. Although the outfit was comfortable, the women couldn't step outdoors without creating an uproar. Finally, Stanton wrote to Anthony, who had complained of the abuse she received for wearing bloomers, "It is not wise, Susan, to use up so much energy and feeling that way. You can put [your energies] to better use." And so the "bloomer costume" became history.

Meanwhile, Susan Anthony was busy. In her first campaign she asked the New York state legislature for three reforms: the right of women to control their own earnings; the right to be guardians of their own children; and the vote. She created a statewide organization of sixty women to promote these reforms. People were stunned to see these unchaperoned women traveling alone from town to town, knocking on every door. After 6,000 signatures had been collected, Susan Anthony presented them to the state judiciary committee. In spite of her eloquent speech, she was told she did not have enough signatures.

Undaunted, she set out again on Christmas Day, 1854. From one town to the next she trooped, making speeches and distributing petitions and literature. Since she was short of money, she did everything herself, from arranging for meeting halls to supervising lights, ushers, announcements, and programs. On one occasion her feet were frostbitten, but she did not stop. She had someone carry her on stage so that she could speak.

Stanton, who had eight children, watched the progress of the campaign

This nineteenth century lithograph depicts a woman wearing the distinctive "Bloomer costume."

from the sidelines. Yet she was every bit as committed to the cause as Susan Anthony. From their mutual admiration had come a bond that was to last their entire lives. While Stanton seemed to be the unspoken leader of the two, they brought equally vital talents to the woman's cause. Anthony did the difficult groundwork of organizing and traveling; Stanton stayed home, drafting the petitions, appeals, and speeches.

The work of Lucy Stone was also progressing in Massachusetts. As one of the planners of the Worcester Convention, Lucy continued her speech-making and each year conducted a petition campaign. "Lucy and I and Antoinette Brown are the work horses of the movement," remarked Susan Anthony in the early 1850s. Since all three were unmarried and had no other demands, they could work around the clock.

That situation changed in 1855, when Lucy wed Henry Blackwell, the younger brother of America's first woman doctor. Henry was in total sympathy with the woman's movement, so Lucy had hoped to continue working just as hard for woman's rights after her marriage. But despite her best intentions, married life and the birth of her daughter distanced her from the movement for several years. The same thing happened to Antoinette Brown, who married and had six children.

From 1855 on, Anthony was left doing the heavy work single-handedly. She was soon elected to the National Committee of the Anti-Slavery Society. Grateful for her assistance, the abolitionist leaders began providing more financial support to the woman's movement.

In 1860, after years of pressure, the New York legislature passed a bill providing women with the right to sue in court and to collect their own wages. It also gave widows the same right to inheritance and guardianship of their children as widowers. Nor was progress limited to New York. Only twelve years had passed after Seneca Falls, but a revolution had taken place in people's attitudes. Woman's abilities were being recognized. Their right to appear in public was no longer questioned. Their need for legal protection was being met.

The woman's movement was quieter during the Civil War. The leaders of the abolitionist and woman's rights movements joined together and directed their energies to winning the war and freeing the slaves. The price of lowering the banner for women, though, was high. In 1862 the New York legislature withdrew most of what women had gained in 1860. Yet, the war had a positive long-term effect on American women. It drew them out of their homes to help in the war effort or to run the businesses the men had left behind. When the war ended, many were unwilling to resume lives of domesticity.

During the war Susan Anthony had traveled throughout New York with a petition demanding an end to slavery. She had been able to collect 400,000 signatures and raise $3,000 for the Union war effort. When the war ended and the slaves were finally freed, she felt that the abolitionists should help her to revive the woman's rights movement. But the abolitionists were more concerned about what would happen to the former slaves. They were free, but without the right to vote, and they would be at the mercy of revenge-seeking white Southerners. Wendell Phillips, an abolitionist leader, asked the women to delay launching their crusade until blacks had the vote.

Lucy Stone understood his point about not confusing the two issues. She was willing to wait. But not Susan Anthony. Having put aside her life's work for five years, she was in no mood to wait longer. Why should illiterate men be allowed to vote when highly educated women could not?

In the spring of 1867 the state of Kansas put two proposed state constitutional amendments to a vote. One would give blacks the vote; the other would give women the vote. By now, leaders of the woman's movement had met and reorganized themselves into the Equal Rights Association, with the twin goals of winning the vote for women and blacks. Representing this new organization, Lucy Stone and her husband, Henry Blackwell, traveled to Kansas to campaign for the two amendments during the spring and summer of 1867. Travel was hard and housing scarce. The governor of Kansas, who supported the amendments, helped to smooth their way, and the abolitionists sent money for campaign literature.

That fall, Susan Anthony and Elizabeth Stanton replaced Lucy Stone and Henry Blackwell in Kansas. By then, the situation had changed. The two amendments, which linked women and blacks together in people's minds, had begun to hurt each other. Moreover, the abolitionist money had dried up. To make matters worse, the governor was about to lose the election and couldn't afford to support unpopular causes.

Just as Anthony and Stanton began to feel completely discouraged, they met George Train. Train, an eccentric millionaire, wanted to be President of the United States. Although he supported woman's suffrage, he was a "copperhead," a Northerner who had opposed the Civil War. Thus, he was disliked by the abolitionists. In fact, few people took George Train seriously. When he offered financial support to Anthony and Stanton, they were too desperate to refuse.

The three began to travel around Kansas together. "You ought to have a woman's paper," George Train suggested to Anthony one day. There was nothing she wanted more than a newspaper devoted to the woman's cause. And so, with Mr. Train's money, the *Revolution* was launched. Its motto was "Men, their rights and nothing more; Women, their rights and nothing less."

Lucy Stone was very upset when she heard the news of Anthony and Stanton's link with George Train. Since Stanton always attracted large crowds to her speeches, Lucy felt that Train was using the two women to further his presidential ambitions. She quickly put a notice in the newspaper saying that Anthony and Stanton were not touring as representatives of the Equal Rights Association.

Susan Anthony was furious. "I *am* the Equal Rights Association. Not a soul of you amounts to shucks except myself," she huffed.

At the 1869 Equal Rights Convention Elizabeth Stanton was denounced by her old friend Frederick Douglass for her ties with George Train. Delegates were faced with a difficult problem— the needs of women and the needs of

— 1820 — February 15 — 1895 —

blacks. Finally, most of them agreed that the crisis of Reconstruction made it necessary to emphasize suffrage for blacks rather than suffrage for women. The Equal Rights Association passed a resolution supporting the Fifteenth Amendment. Since this amendment provided for black male suffrage only, it put the leaders of the woman's movement into the position of backing something that excluded women.

This was too much for Anthony. She called together a group of women who were also outraged, and a new organization, the National Woman Suffrage Association, was formed. Its sole purpose was to secure the vote for women. In changing the woman's movement to a suffrage movement, Anthony sepa-

Susan B. Anthony posed for this picture in 1898, marking the 50th anniversary of the Seneca Falls Convention.

rated it forever from the abolitionist cause and gave it not only a clear goal, but also new energy.

Lucy Stone realized that the Equal Rights Association was dead. Distrusting Susan Anthony, she formed a second woman's suffrage group, the American Woman's Suffrage Association. She even launched a competitive newspaper, the *Woman's Journal*. Meanwhile, Susan Anthony's newspaper, the *Revolution*, proved too radical for most women and folded after two years.

From 1870 on, Lucy Stone quietly managed the *Woman's Journal* and ran the American Woman's Suffrage Association. At the same time, Elizabeth Stanton and Susan Anthony, leading the smaller National Woman Suffrage Association, went from one blaze of publicity to the next as they sought to arouse public support for woman's suffrage.

A GALLERY OF AMERICAN WOMEN FIRSTS

The ten American women shown here each achieved a significant "first" in a specific field. Whether that achievement took place in the field of literature, business, politics, art, or science, each of these women contributed something of value to her nation—and to the world. What makes their achievements even more remarkable is that all but two of them were born before all American women won the vote.

Martha Washington (1732–1802), the first American woman to be pictured on a postage stamp.

Social worker Jane Addams (1860–1935), the first American woman to receive a Nobel Peace Prize (1931).

Madame C. J. Walker (1867–1919) turned $1.50 in capital into a cosmetics empire, becoming the first American woman millionaire.

Jeanette Rankin (1880–1973), the first woman elected to the U.S. Congress—from Montana in 1917.

Frances Perkins (1882–1965), appointed Secretary of Labor by President Franklin Roosevelt (also shown) in 1933, was the first woman cabinet member.

Author Pearl S. Buck (1892–1973), the first American woman to win the Nobel Prize for Literature (1938).

Golda Meir (1898–1978) became the first former American woman to lead a foreign government when she was elected prime minister of Israel in 1969.

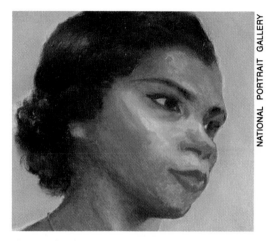

Opera singer Marian Anderson (1902–), the first woman awarded the Presidential Medal of Freedom (1963).

Sandra Day O'Connor (1930–), the first woman justice of the U.S. Supreme Court (1981).

Sally Ride (1951–), the first American woman astronaut. In 1983 she became the first American woman to go into space.

3

DECADES OF HOPE AND CONFLICT

As the national election of 1872 approached, the names of new voters throughout the country were added to voter registration lists. But the most surprising name of all appeared in Rochester, New York: Susan B. Anthony.

Susan Anthony did not think she would be allowed to vote. She wanted to make a point. The recent passage of the Fourteenth and Fifteenth Amendments to the United States Constitution had given full rights of citizenship to blacks. Yet neither amendment had mentioned blacks by name. They had stated only that the right of citizens to vote could not be denied on account of race. If citizens could vote, Anthony had responded, why couldn't women vote? Women were citizens.

This engraving shows women at the polls in Wyoming during the election of 1888. Wyoming gave women the vote in 1869, when it was still a territory.

When Anthony, her sister, and several other women entered the shoemaker's shop in Rochester to register in the city's Eighth Ward, the registrars were astonished. But they made no attempt to stop the women from adding their names to the list of eligible voters.

Registering to vote was one thing; actually casting ballots was quite another. When word spread that Susan Anthony and fifteen other women had voted in the national election, government officials felt they had to do something. So, on Thanksgiving Day, the United States Chief Marshall came to Anthony's door. When she refused to answer his summons, he arrested her and the other women. As the "ringleader," Susan Anthony was the only one brought to trial.

With her trial set for May 1873, Anthony spent the next few months trying to rally the public to her side. Her defense was the Fourteenth Amendment. If the amendment had given her the

Louisa Swain, the first woman to cast a vote after the Wyoming Territory gave women suffrage in 1869.

right to vote, she argued, how could she be accused of breaking the law? Before her trial, no court had dealt with the issue.

The trial was unfair. From the opening day it was clear that the judge wanted to convict her. First, he agreed with the district attorney that women were unfit to speak in courts of law. Next, he dismissed the jury. Then he found her guilty of breaking the law when she voted. Finally, he asked whether she had anything to say. Furious that she hadn't been allowed to defend herself earlier, Anthony angrily said that she wouldn't pay a penny of her $100 fine.

Before the trial, newspapers had always described Susan Anthony as a humorless spinster. But people were so disgusted by her unfair trial that even the most conservative papers applauded her. In 1874 she was named one of America's best-known women.

When Anthony's newspaper, the *Revolution*, folded, she was left $10,000 in debt. To pay this off, she joined Elizabeth Stanton on the paid lecture circuit. Stanton, lecturing to put her children through college, was a real crowd-pleaser. But people also came to admire Anthony for her selflessness and frankness. Although she had paid off her entire debt by 1876, she continued to lecture, canceling only two engagements in twenty years on the circuit.

As Susan Anthony's fame grew, her National Suffrage group prospered. While Lucy Stone's organization focused on state suffrage, the NWSA campaigned for a federal suffrage amendment. Every year, Anthony spent time in Washington lobbying congressmen. Through her efforts, the proposed amendment was discussed in committee hearings. Anthony also attended all of the party conventions, vainly trying to get Republicans and Democrats to adopt a woman's suffrage plank in their platforms. The Democratic South was opposed to the amendment, because they didn't want black women voting. And neither party was willing to double the number of voters without knowing which party the new voters would support. But by the end of the 1880s, the Anthony Amendment (as it was called) had won the support of many citizens.

Meanwhile, woman's suffrage was advancing on other fronts. When the Territory of Wyoming was established in 1869, Esther Morriss, a rugged frontier woman, called together a group of community leaders. She argued that women should be given the vote in the new territory. The men at the meeting agreed with her. On the Western frontier, where women braved the hardships of the wilderness equally with men, old prejudices seemed out of place. A suffrage bill managed to slip through both houses of the territory legislature and was signed into law by the governor.

Some people feared violence would erupt when women actually tried to vote. The first brave woman to do so was a seventy-five-year-old Quaker grandmother, Louisa Swain, who marched into a polling booth in Laramie, Wyoming. No one stopped her. Other women followed. Both political parties were so anxious to win women's votes that they made sure the voting went smoothly.

When Wyoming became a state in 1890, Washington lawmakers pressed for a repeal of the woman's suffrage law. But Wyoming's leaders declared they would rather stay out of the Union for a hundred years than change the law. Thus, Wyoming became the first state with woman's suffrage. It was followed quickly by Colorado and Idaho, and by Utah in 1896. These western victories were a sign that the work of Susan Anthony, the *Woman's Journal*, and the two rival woman's suffrage associations was beginning to pay off.

After the Civil war, new prosperity freed many women to work for social causes outside their homes. The most popular middle-class woman's issue was temperance—the movement to end the sale of alcohol. Few laws protected women and children from the abuses of drunken husbands and fathers. After the war, alcohol production increased, and since taxes on alcohol were an important source of money, the government ignored the family problems caused by alcohol.

In 1873 a hundred women in Hillsboro, Ohio, marched from their church to the nearest saloon. There they knelt down and prayed that the saloonkeeper would get out of the liquor business. After newspapers ran stories about the campaign, the saloon closed. Soon liquor stores and saloons all over the country were getting the same treatment. Because there were many prominent women in each community kneeling all day on grimy saloon floors, the authorities were unwilling to arrest them. Thus, the "Woman's War," as newspapers called it, went on through 1874, resulting in the temporary closing of 3,000 saloons. These successes soon led to the formation of the Woman's National Christian Temperance Union, or WCTU.

In 1879 Francis Willard became President of the WCTU. In order to fight alcohol interests, she decided, women needed the vote, which she called the "Home Protection Ballot." Thus, the

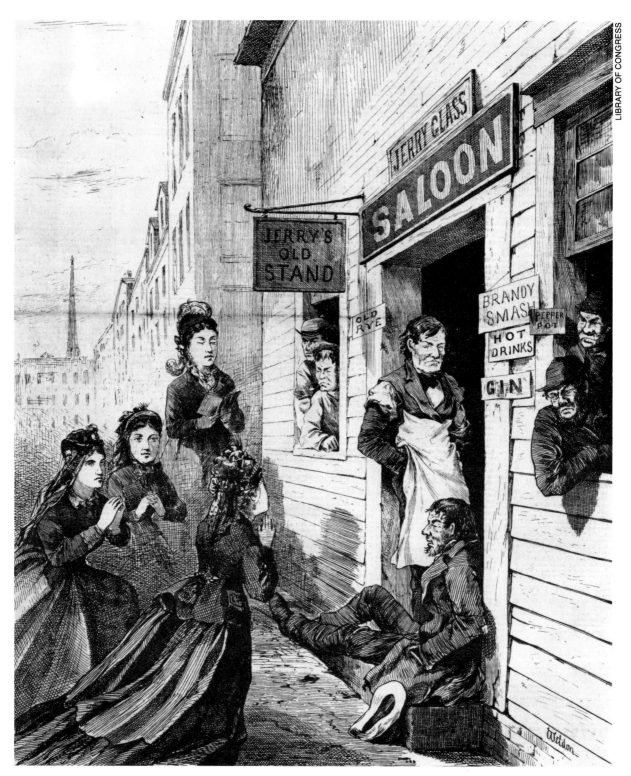

Many American women joined the temperance movement in the latter half of the nineteenth century. Praying in or near a saloon was a favorite tactic of temperance activists.

WCTU joined the suffrage movement. With it came large numbers of local workers, more money, and the support of masses of ordinary, middle-class American women who had never supported suffrage before. This new strength helped the fight for woman's suffrage spread to several more states. To change a state's constitution to include woman's suffrage, however, meant holding a referendum, a direct appeal to the voters at a state election.

In 1890 just such a referendum was part of the election in South Dakota. Saloonkeepers and liquor dealers were scared of granting the vote to women, whom they saw as do-gooders who would vote to end the sale of alcohol in the state. They organized themselves to defeat the suffrage referendum. They rounded up all the immigrants they could find—many of whom couldn't read or speak English—and paid them for their votes. Often, the bribes were handed out in full view of those guarding the polls.

Susan Anthony, seventy years old and in poor health, came to South Dakota and campaigned hard for the referendum. "Better lose me than lose a state," she said. But the pro-alcohol forces were just too strong. The South Dakota referendum was lost. Many people were angered by the corruption and fraud at the polls, however, and woman's suffrage thus gained increasing sympathy.

During the 1870s and 1880s the two national woman's suffrage organizations had used different strategies to win the vote for women. One was Lucy Stone's American Woman's Suffrage Association, which fought at the state level. The other was the National Woman Suffrage Association of Susan Anthony and Elizabeth Stanton, which worked for national suffrage. By the end of the 1880s the three "mothers" of the movement were ready to be reunited. They were older, and Stanton, the oldest, had moved to England to live with her daughter, Harriet Stanton Blatch. All three knew it was time for new leaders to take charge.

In 1889 the two rival suffrage groups merged into one group, the National-American Association. At Susan Anthony's insistence, Elizabeth Stanton was named as the united organization's first president. But Stanton resigned in 1892, and that same year Lucy Stone died. Susan Anthony took over the National-American's leadership. Anthony, who had become the outstanding figure of the suffrage movement, remained president until 1900.

Throughout the 1890s, however, Anthony was seldom without her able assistant and close friend, Anna Shaw. A brilliant woman and a gifted speaker, Shaw had grown up in poverty in rural Michigan. She had been a teacher before putting herself through both theology school and medical school. After meeting Susan Anthony, she was so impressed she had decided nothing she could do in her life could be more important than helping to win the vote for women.

In 1894 the biggest suffrage referen-

Four Western states gave women the vote between 1890 and 1896. Here, a Colorado woman celebrates in 1893, when that state adopted woman's suffrage.

dum campaign of the century took place in California. At first, suffrage seemed sure to win. Not only had the Republican and Populist parties come out for it, but all the newspapers favored it as well. A total of $19,000 in campaign funds was raised, largely by working women who saved their earnings to buy two-dollar portraits of Susan Anthony and Anna Shaw. Women spoke for suffrage throughout the state, and copies of the *Woman's Journal* were distributed everywhere. Susan Anthony traveled west, crossing California by train, making speeches at every stop.

But the opposition organized and grew powerful. Liquor dealers ran ad-vertisements, mounted doorbell campaigns, got out the immigrant vote, and carried registration books into workplaces. Under secret pressure, the Republicans and Populists withdrew their support. The state was lost.

Despite the loss of California, the 1890s was a fairly successful decade for suffrage. Two states were won, and two territories that had suffrage became states. Yet all four of these western states were small in population. Susan Anthony, meanwhile, had gone to live with her sister in Rochester. From that distance she could no longer keep up pressure on Congress for a federal suffrage amendment. Without a strong national organization, women carried on the struggle for suffrage at state and local levels.

Anthony realized that the time had come for her to retire. She wanted Anna Shaw to succeed her as president of the National-American, but another contender, Carrie Chapman Catt, had emerged.

Carrie Chapman Catt, a former newspaper editor from Iowa, had been a delegate to the first convention of the newly merged National American in 1890. She had also taken part in the South Dakota campaign. Although she had almost died of typhoid there, she had proved herself to the movement's leaders. In 1894 she led the victorious referendum campaign in Colorado.

In 1895 Susan Anthony appointed Carrie Catt president of the Organization Committee for the National-American. Within two years she had

Belva Lockwood, the first woman lawyer to argue before the Supreme Court, ran for president in 1884 and 1888 as the National Equal Rights party's candidate. Here, men of the "Belva Lockwood Club" ridicule her in a political parade.

opened a New York office and had fourteen full-time organizers working in the field. She saw that every state and territory was brought into the association, including ten states with no previous suffrage organization. Through her leadership, Idaho became a suffrage state in 1896, and suffrage conventions had been held in Iowa, in South Dakota, and in every county in Illinois.

Catt was an effective leader because she was extremely intelligent and had exceptional organizational capabilities. Also, she was married to George Catt, a very rich man. That was one of the reasons she, and not Anna Shaw, became president of the National-American Association when Susan Anthony re-

signed in 1900. Having money of one's own had become almost a necessity for running an organization with such a limited budget.

Under Catt's leadership, state suffrage leaders became more skilled. Also, the National Association grew more prosperous. When a suffrage referendum came up in New Hampshire, Catt traveled to Concord with fifteen speakers. No one could have worked harder. She spoke five days a week, wading through snowdrifts up to her knees to reach voters. But big business, organized crime, and the entire male political structure were against the interests of women. New Hampshire was lost.

In 1904 Carrie Catt resigned the pres-

WOMAN'S PLACE IN THE CHRISTIAN WORLD:

SUPERIOR MORALLY, INFERIOR MENTALLY, TO MAN— NOT QUALIFIED FOR MEDICINE OR LAW—THE CONTRARIETY AND HARMONY OF THE SEXES.*

By W. W. PARKER, M. D., of Richmond, Va.,
Honorary Fellow and Ex-President of Medical Society of Virginia.

God having finished this splendid world, placed at its grand arched gateway imperial man, stately and stalwart, with will and wisdom stamped upon his lofty brow. In his stout belt we see the broad sword and woodman's axe, and at his feet the plow and pruning-hook. In his right hand he holds the roll of chartered rights, of dominion over field and forest, land and sea. By his left he holds the soft, white hand of blue-eyed, fair-haired Eve, his royal queen, radiant in beauty, gentle, timid in manner, and in every movement the perfection of grace. She holds to her bosom the embryo race, the pledge of mutual love. Her mission is to rear the offspring and ever fan the flame of piety, patriotism and love upon the sacred altar of home.

It is of her, and her holy mission, I desire especially to speak; of her duties, responsibilities, and peculiarities; to differentiate them, if I can, from those of her consort man, and to fix her true place in the Christian world.

---

* Read at a meeting of the Medical Society of Virginia at Alleghany Springs, Va., September 13–15, 1892.

A part of the above Essay was published anonymously in the *Dispatch* February, 1891.

This cartoon humorously depicts Elizabeth Stanton and Susan Anthony, the leaders of the National-American Association.

idency of the National-American in order to help her ailing husband travel to Europe. Anna Shaw took her place. Susan Anthony, who lived long enough to see her favorite take the reins of the suffrage organization, died soon afterward at the age of eighty-six. As it turned out, Shaw was not the kind of woman the movement needed to move it forward. Many of her ideas were old-fashioned. Whenever any of the state organizations

This 1892 "report" shows the sentimental, simplistic way in which most nineteenth-century men thought of women.

suggested new ideas or approaches to the national organization, Shaw reacted with suspicion.

Harriet Blatch, the daughter of Elizabeth Stanton, returned to America from England. She was glad that her mother had not lived to see what had become of her life's work. No new suffrage states had been added in eleven years, and the federal amendment was dead. True, the idea of women voting had become widely respected, but that was the problem: because so many believed in it, few were willing to fight for it. A cause that had once been exciting had stopped moving ahead.

4

THE NEW VIGOR

In America, the woman's suffrage movement was going nowhere. But that was not the case in England. There, Emmeline Pankhurst and her suffragettes were making waves.

Emmeline Pankhurst had founded the Women's Social and Political Union. The group wanted Britain's political parties to introduce woman's suffrage to Parliament. It held large outdoor meetings to attract new members, and it was the first suffrage group to appeal to working-class women.

One day in 1905 the foreign minister made a political appearance. Several women from Pankhurst's group attended. One of them asked him what he planned to do about woman's suffrage. When he ignored her, she unfurled a suffrage flag and asked again. Finally,

This cartoon shows William Jennings Bryan, Democratic candidate for president in 1896, 1900, and 1908, raising a woman's suffrage flag. Bryan was one of the first major politicians to support suffrage.

after she refused to sit down, the guards escorted her, struggling, into the street. She and another woman immediately formed a protest meeting. They were then arrested and jailed.

The incident made headlines all over England. It became clear to Emmeline Pankhurst that a small amount of disorderly conduct would focus the public's attention on suffrage. The English suffragette movement was born. It used direct political action and sensational acts to keep suffrage in the public's eye. When one of Pankhurst's supporters threw herself in front of the king's horse as it was winning the Derby, there were headlines. When a group of suffragettes paraded outside the prime minister's residence, there were headlines. When the government jailed women for breaking the law, force-feeding them after they went on hunger strikes, there were headlines. Most British supporters of woman's suffrage, however, were horrified by Pankhurst's methods.

Not Harriet Stanton Blatch. When

After the American suffrage movement revived, pro-suffrage parades became common in many American communities. This one took place on Long Island, New York, in 1913.

she returned to New York from England, she met with a group of people to plan the revival of the American suffrage movement. She was an admirer of Emmeline Pankhurst's, and believed a new, politically minded suffrage group was needed. She felt it must appeal to working women, since they stood to gain the most from suffrage. In January 1907 the Woman's Political Union was formed.

That year Blatch and some trade-union women went to the annual suffrage discussion in the New York State legislature. Outdoor public meetings were held in New York City. By mid–1908 the organization had 19,000 members. Blatch campaigned by trolley throughout the state to spread the word

about the cause. In 1909 she opened an office in New York City and ran a campaign to win state lawmakers to the suffrage cause. Her efforts resulted, in 1910, in a suffrage bill being debated in both houses of the state legislature for the first time in fifteen years.

Harriet Blatch also invited the leaders of the National-American Association to join suffrage leaders in a huge Fifth Avenue parade. The National-American rode up the avenue in cars in "a blur of yellow," the suffrage color. After 1910 there was a suffrage parade every year in New York, each one larger and more colorful than the last.

By now, Carrie Catt had also returned from Europe. She did not sympathize with Emmeline Pankhurst. But she was also interested in organizing a new suffrage movement. She feared that Pankhurst's influence might produce an extremist party in America. Catt formed the Woman Suffrage Party in New York City and organized it into 63 election districts and 2,127 precincts, each with a captain. It was the first attempt to unite all suffrage groups to win over a major city, and it created a sensation. Suffrage balls and art exhibits were held, suffrage bazaars and restaurants opened, and suffrage posters were put up in seven languages.

Still, it wasn't enough to persuade the politicians to introduce suffrage in the state legislature. Thus, the second annual Fifth Avenue Parade in 1911 became a protest march. It ended in huge outdoor meetings, with 10,000 people crowding into Union Square alone.

Had the suffrage movement become an invincible force? In the far West, it began to seem that way. Oregon became a suffrage state. And in 1911, after a campaign that included 10,000 workers plus hundreds of advertisements and suffrage parades, California was won at last.

But the California victory also spurred on the opponents of suffrage. When both Michigan and Ohio had suffrage referenda in 1912, optimism ran high. Funded by liquor companies, the opposition worked hard, drilling immigrants on how to vote, stuffing ballot boxes, and reporting false vote counts. The referenda lost in both states. And

The leaders of the suffrage movement march down Fifth Avenue in 1917, the year New York was won for suffrage.

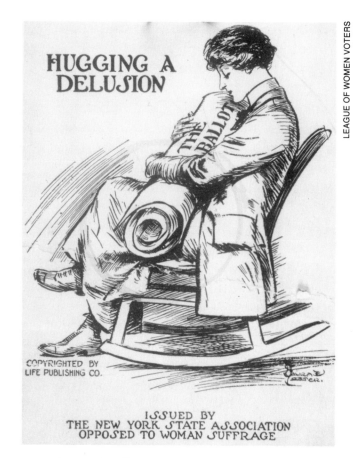

An anti-suffrage group issued this pamphlet in 1917. Within three years, however, the "delusion" of women having the vote was a reality.

in 1915, despite a huge effort by suffrage groups, New York lost another referendum.

Running more referenda campaigns in more states seemed hopeless. Those who did not want women to vote were just too powerful. In the South, white women had asked lawmakers for the vote in order to maintain white rule. But white men did not want to share political power with anyone, neither blacks nor women. So, in the South, poll taxes and other voting measures were instituted to make it harder for everyone to

vote, and referenda on woman's suffrage never even came up. Elsewhere in the nation, executives of railroad, oil, and manufacturing companies looked at women as dreamers and do-gooders. These businessmen sided with the alcohol interests. If women could vote, these men believed, they would make the sale of alcohol illegal. Also, they might kill prosperity by forcing businesses to spend more money on caring for their workers. All these "anti" forces put pressure on state lawmakers. Sometimes bribes were used, but often it was enough to threaten the legislators by saying they wouldn't receive support in the next election.

The time had come for the suffrage movement to change tactics. Luckily, there was a woman who stood ready to lead the way.

Alice Paul was the youngest and most modern of all the great suffrage leaders. She was completely selfless, a hard worker who had the knack of getting others to work hard, too. She was raised a Quaker, had graduated from Swarthmore College, and had earned a Ph.D. In England, where she had gone to complete her education, she had become a follower of Emmeline Pankhurst.

Returning to America in 1912, Paul set out for Washington. With her was Lucy Burns, another young American who had been swept up in England's suffragette movement. The two agreed that the shortest way to the vote was a federal amendment. Alice Paul was named the Washington leader of the

National-American. Her job was to establish a Washington lobby for the amendment and to win national support for it.

In January 1913, when President-elect Woodrow Wilson arrived in Washington for his inauguration, he found few people there to greet him.

"Where are the crowds?" he asked.

"Over on the Avenue watching the suffrage parade," he was told.

On Pennsylvania Avenue 5,000 women were marching. Since a Democratic president and Congress were to be sworn in the next day, thousands of Democrats were in town. Enraged, they shouted obscene remarks, spat, and threw burning cigar butts at the marching women. Fighting broke out. Alice Paul was thrilled at the publicity that resulted.

President Wilson said that he didn't know enough about the issue to say whether he favored women having the vote. Alice Paul led several groups of women to talk to him. When these visits produced nothing, a massive demonstration followed. Delegates from all over the country brought petitions to Washington. Then, with the approval of Anna Shaw, Alice Paul formed the Congressional Union to lobby Congress. Within months, workers had been sent all over the country, and congressmen were being bombarded by letters and visits from suffragists. Despite the constant pressure, President Wilson and the Democratic Congress failed to act. Alice Paul decided that in the 1914 election all Democratic candidates, par-

Twelve Reasons Why Mothers Should Have The Vote

Better Babies—Better Homes—Better Schools.

1. BECAUSE the mother's business is home-making and child-rearing, and the child and the home are the greatest asset of the nation.

2. BECAUSE the welfare of the child is affected by the laws of the State as well as the rules of the home.

3. BECAUSE there are just as many home interests in the government as there are business interests and the mother is primarily the custodian of these home interests.

4. BECAUSE the lowest death rate of babies in the world is in New Zealand, the country where mothers have had the vote the longest. In that country, the government sends out nurses to every town, village and country district, to instruct and aid mothers in the care of their babies. Young girls are taught baby hygiene and feeding.

5. BECAUSE the banner baby state, California, an equal suffrage state, has the highest birth rate and a very low death rate. (The lowest death rate of babies in the United States is in the city of Seattle, Washington State, where women vote.

6. BECAUSE children have better school facilities where mothers vote. Washington, an equal suffrage state, is the banner state in education. State-wide compulsory education and child labor laws put every child under fourteen years of age in school, where women vote.

7. BECAUSE girls have equal educational opportunities with boys from Kindergarten to State University, where women vote.

8. BECAUSE the moral conditions of our country are regulated by law. Should not mothers have a say about the dangers and temptations which surround their boys and girls?

9. BECAUSE girls of tender age are better protected by law where mothers vote. The age of consent is highest in the suffrage states.

10. BECAUSE mothers are equal guardians with fathers of their children in the states which have had suffrage the longest.

11. BECAUSE widowed mothers are protected by mother's pensions in the states where women vote.

12. BECAUSE it is just, it is expedient, and has proven a good governmental poilicy for mothers to have a voice in the laws which control themselves and their children.

A suffrage group issued this pamphlet, which gives twelve reasons why women with children should have the vote.

ticularly those in the eight states where women could vote, would be opposed.

Suffragists who felt a strong party loyalty were against this policy. Carrie Catt and the other National-American leaders were upset as well. They felt that the Congressional Union had become too independent. A split took place. Alice Paul formed her own organization, calling it the Woman's Party. On the other side were Anna Shaw, Carrie Catt, and the National-American,

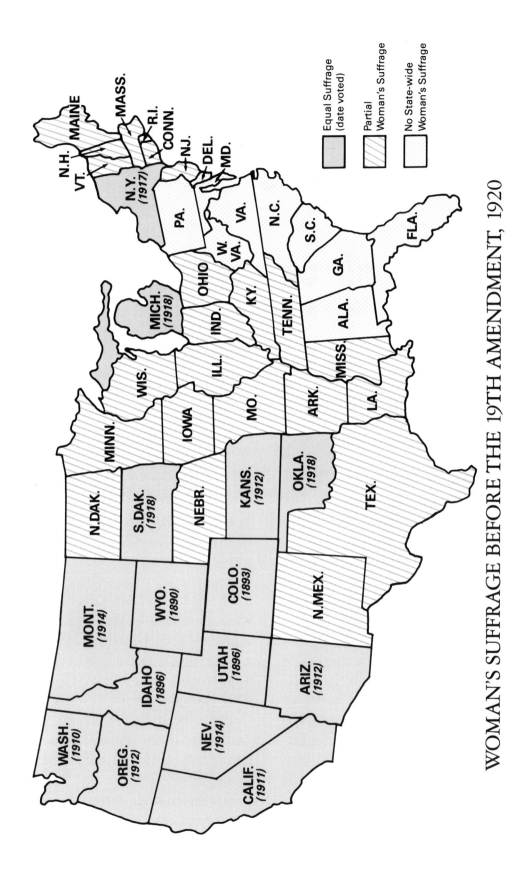

WOMAN'S SUFFRAGE BEFORE THE 19TH AMENDMENT, 1920

Equal Suffrage (date voted)

Partial Woman's Suffrage

No State-wide Woman's Suffrage

which was the more widely accepted group.

But Alice Paul had her own share of loyal supporters, among them some very prominent women. A wealthy socialite, Mrs. O.H.P. Belmont, paid for a new headquarters located just across Lafayette Square from the White House. From here, Alice Paul arranged her publicity campaigns. In 1915 she organized a motorcade from San Francisco to Washington that carried a petition 18,000 feet long, with 500,000 names.

By now President Wilson had come out in favor of suffrage, as long as it was won state by state. The Anthony Amendment, as the proposed suffrage amendment had come to be called, had been voted on in both the House of Representatives and the Senate, but it had lost by a big margin. During the 1916 presidential campaign, the Republican candidate, Charles Evans Hughes, said he supported suffrage. President Wilson merely predicted that one day it would be the law of the land. Disgusted by this meaningless remark, the Woman's Party again campaigned against Wilson and the Democrats.

Alice Paul grew more impatient. In December 1916, while the president was giving his yearly address to Congress, a huge yellow banner was suddenly dropped form the balcony. It read, "Mr. President, What Will You Do For Woman's Suffrage?"

On January 10, 1917, a dozen women holding suffrage banners and placards moved in single file from the Woman's Party headquarters and stationed themselves at the gates of the White House. When the first group grew tired, a fresh shift took their place. Day after day they came, standing on hot bricks when the weather grew frigid. That April the United States entered World War I. Alice Paul was a Quaker and didn't believe in war. She declared that the work of the Woman's Party would go on as usual. She pointed out that it was two-faced of President Wilson to lead the country into a fight for democracy overseas while denying women the right to vote in their own country.

Most Americans, as well as other suffrage groups, felt the Woman's Party was being unpatriotic. That June a mob attacked the White House pickets. Alice Paul refused to stop. The government couldn't tolerate rioting in front of the White House, so, finally, the pickets were arrested and jailed.

Reports about conditions in the jail where the women were held shocked many people—there were worms found in prison food, and there were filth, rats, and mice. Outside the White House, the picketing continued. That fall, even worse stories came from the Occoquan Workhouse. One woman had been thrown into her cell so roughly she lost consciousness. Another, over seventy years old, was dragged across a courtyard. Lucy Burns had been handcuffed with her arms over her head and left that way overnight. Finally, Alice Paul herself was arrested and taken to the district jail, where she joined seventy-five other women in three tiers of windowless cells. After going on a hunger strike and being force-fed, she grew so weak she had to be sent to the prison hospital.

Although the Woman's Party had never been popular, news of the prison conditions and brutal treatment of the women horrified people. Women began coming long distances to take turns in the picket line and in jail. Contributions flowed into the Woman's Party. It was time for the government to retreat. On December 3, 1917, the pickets were all released.

In Congress, the attitude toward woman's suffrage had begun to change. Temperance propaganda had resulted in a national prohibition amendment that, if passed, would ban the manufacture and sale of alcohol. So the liquor lobby was busy fighting prohibition rather than suffrage. By now the National-American Association was also seeking a federal amendment. In fact, while Alice Paul had been grabbing headlines, Carrie Catt had been quietly making some brilliant plans. Largely through her efforts, the U.S. House of Representatives was ready to vote on a suffrage amendment.

Carrie Catt had replaced the elderly Anna Shaw as President of the National-American in 1915. Using her own fortune as well as the promise of $2 million from the estate of Mrs. Frank Leslie, she brought the organization to life. The first assault from the reorganized group was felt at the 1916 national political party conventions. The women drew up a suffrage plank that they wanted included in both party's platforms. They circulated it among political leaders and convention delegates. In Chicago and St. Louis, the convention sites, huge rallies and parades were held. But both conventions ended in a compromise, favoring woman's suffrage but deciding it ought to be done by the states. At the close of the Democratic Convention, Carrie Catt announced an emergency convention of the National-American Association in Atlantic City, New Jersey, that fall.

In Atlantic City, Carrie Catt outlined her "secret plan." To get a federal amendment, suffrage forces in every state would be coordinated to put pressure on congressmen at the same time.

By now, in addition to the states with full suffrage, there were states with partial suffrage. Through the years, women had been granted the right to vote in certain local elections, such as elections for school boards. This right had been given to them not through statewide referenda but rather by their own state legislatures. In 1914 Illinois went one step further: The state legislature gave women the right to vote for president.

Carrie Catt said that in suffrage states women should concentrate on pressuring their congressmen for a federal amendment. In states without any kind of suffrage, women should press for anything they could get from their state legislatures. In states that had municipal suffrage, women should campaign for the presidential vote, as they had done in Illinois. Success, said Catt, would depend on secrecy and speed. If suffrage workers were doing so much in

Above: Woman ambulance drivers pose beside their vehicles during World War I.

Right: This sentimental painting shows a World War I nurse. Thousands of American women served in the armed forces during the war, mostly as nurses or clerical workers.

so many states, the opponents wouldn't know where to direct their efforts. When she added that $1 million would be needed, enthusiasm was so great that $800,000 was pledged immediately. The National-American then hired two hundred full-time organizers.

Two centers were opened, one in New York, where the state's efforts were directed, and another in Washington, where the national effort was organized. In Washington, files on each congressman were carefully researched and kept, outlining each man's strengths, weaknesses, and interests. Using this information, well-trained suffrage lobbyists would call on the congressman, taking care to be polite and brief, but persuasive.

During the war, Carrie Catt took a different view from Alice Paul. She believed that all women must be part of the war effort. She herself joined the Woman's Committee of the Council of National Defense. But she also believed that the suffrage work must go on. Through the efforts of her group, presidential suffrage was granted by six state legislatures by the end of 1917. The most populous state in the nation, New York, was finally won through a referendum in the same year.

The tide had turned. Victory in New York added 43 pro-suffrage votes in the House of Representatives. By the end of 1917 the number of presidential electoral votes in which women had a share had reached 215. When word arrived that the House of Representatives had agreed to vote on a suffrage amendment, Alice Paul took full credit for the victory. But Carrie Catt and her colleagues complained that the Woman's Party had been merely an obstacle. The truth probably lies somewhere in between. Alice Paul's activities put suffrage in the public eye and made the government uncomfortable. But it was the political efforts of the National-

American that made the most progress.

The date set for the vote in the House was January 10, 1918. Research had convinced women that they were 45 votes short of the two-thirds majority needed. Prominent party leaders, including President Wilson, spoke out for the amendment. Women poured into Washington for last-minute meetings with their representatives. The morning of the vote was a tense time. Mr. Ireland of Illinois, who was pro-suffrage, was held up by a train wreck; Mr. Crosser of Ohio was sick in bed; Mr. Barnhart of Indiana was in the hospital; and suddenly, the wife of Mr. Hicks from New York died.

The arguments went on for hours. Then the roll call began. There was Mr. Crosser, having risen from his bed. There was Mr. Hicks, who had left his dead wife. A second role call began. Mr. Barnhart was carried in on a stretcher to vote "yea." Finally, after many roll calls, the suffrage amendment passed by a margin of two votes. Instantly, a chorus of woman's voices broke into song, singing "Praise God from Whom All Blessings Flow."

Many thought the suffrage amendment would easily pass the U.S. Senate. However, it took all of 1918 and half of 1919 before the necessary 64 pro-suffrage votes were gained. Alice Paul grew impatient. Beginning in 1918, there were new demonstrations at the White House. These brought a new wave of imprisonments. President Wilson campaigned hard for the amendment. Even so, when the vote was taken in the Senate on February 10, 1919, the amendment lost by one vote. The following May, the 66th Congress was called into special session. Both houses voted on the issue again. This time suffrage passed the House of Representatives by 304 to 90. Two weeks later it passed the Senate.

It took 14 more months of hard work to win the legislatures of the 36 states needed to ratify the amendment. But in August 1920 the battle was over at last.

In the long struggle for suffrage, women had built a powerful political organization. They had conducted 56 referenda campaigns, 480 campaigns to get state legislatures to submit suffrage amendments to voters, and 277 campaigns to persuade party conventions to introduce suffrage in their platforms.

All because half the population of the United States were forced to prove that they were worthy of becoming voting citizens of their own country.

The 1920s was a decade of progress and change for American women. They had finally won the right to vote.

AFTERWORD

NEW STRUGGLES, NEW GOALS

Has the woman's vote made a difference?

The 1920 passage of the Nineteenth Amendment did not bring about complete equality. But neither did it tear the nation apart, as some opponents of suffrage had predicted it would. Although the women who had led the fight for suffrage were skilled in politics, none of them ran for high political office after the vote was won. If they had, perhaps the history of woman's rights in America since 1920 would have been quite different.

After the amendment was ratified, Alice Paul turned to the economic problems of working women. How could women compete for the same jobs and wages as men? Paul and the Woman's

U.S. Representative Geraldine Ferraro, the first woman to be nominated for the vice-presidency by a major political party, faces Republican vice presidential candidate George Bush in a 1980 campaign debate.

Party began pressing for another amendment on behalf of working women. An Equal Rights Amendment, called the Lucretia Mott amendment, was introduced in Congress in 1923. "Equality of rights under the law shall not be abridged by the United States or by any state on account of sex," it said. It failed to win Congress's approval.

Carrie Catt was more concerned about how women would use their right to vote. As early as 1919, she had suggested that once the vote was won, the National-American Association should become the League of Women Voters. The new organization would help women become informed voters and more effective citizens.

The first task of the League of Women Voters was to get women out to vote. The League set up citizenship schools. It showed women how to mark their ballots. It set up groups to telephone women and remind them to vote. On election day, they babysat and drove women to and from the polls. Yet,

The League of Women Voters was founded to help women exercise their right to vote.

all these efforts helped only a little. Very few women voted during the 1920s. But the League didn't give up. They began printing election leaflets describing the candidates. Later, they established an educational program that showed women how to use political power. The program taught about communities, about zoning, slum clearance, and school board participation. It also taught women about the political process and how they could start reforms and shape events.

When woman's suffrage was first proposed at Seneca Falls, it had been just one of a list of rights Elizabeth Cady Stanton and her friends had wanted. By 1920, in addition to winning the vote, women had also won the right to own and inherit property, to be represented in court, and to share in the custody of their own children. These had been the most bitter complaints in 1848. Clearly, they had come a long way, but they still had far to go.

Most of the gains women have made since 1920 were won by the new, vigorous woman's movement of the late 1960s and 1970s. Like the woman's movement of the nineteenth century, it grew out of a concern for the civil rights of black Americans. Women like Rosa Parks, a black woman who refused to move to the back of a bus (where blacks were supposed to sit) in Montgomery, Alabama, were in the front lines of the battle for civil rights in the 1950s and 1960s. As people throughout the nation struggled to integrate schools and register blacks to vote, the words "freedom" and "equality" were heard everywhere. Slowly, women began to realize that they had some unfinished business to attend to as well.

Other sparks helped ignite the new woman's movement. A spirit of change and idealism was in the air. Many women began devoting their time and energy to social causes. Better birth control methods had been introduced, freeing women from unwanted pregnancies. In 1963 a book called *The Feminine Mystique* by Betty Friedan had a big impact on thousands of middle-class housewives. Friedan argued that educated women were being programmed by the media into lives of homemaking. Unless they had more choices available, she said, many women's lives would always be empty and meaningless.

The new woman's movement was launched. Friedan and a group of other women, plus a few men, founded the National Organization for Women (NOW). It began moving forward on several fronts, including reviving the Equal Rights Amendment, which had been dormant for nearly half a century. More women emerged to lead the movement: Kate Millet, Germaine Greer, and Gloria Steinem, to name just a few. Many of NOW's early ideas were considered extreme, and often its top leaders clashed with each other, but it never lacked vitality.

Women in the 1970s began pursuing careers, not marriages. They entered graduate schools by the thousands. No longer content to be nurses, secretaries, and Sunday School teachers, they wanted to be doctors, lawyers, and priests as well. To reach these goals, they were willing to battle the entire male establishment. New laws, including the Equal Pay Act of 1964, had made it difficult for employers to discriminate against women employees. Also,

Above: During World War II, millions of American women poured into factories to take the place of male workers serving in the armed forces.

Right: Betty Friedan's book The Feminine Mystique *inspired many American women to demand full equality and new opportunities.*

women were showing a new willingness to take legal action against unfair employers and to go to court whenever their rights were ignored. By the end of the 1970s, women had made much progress toward taking their places alongside men in what were once considered exclusively male jobs and professions.

After women won the vote, the politicians of the 1920s worried that women might go to the polls in one powerful special-interest block, but this has never happened. Women, like men, tend to vote along party lines. Some issues, such as abortion or day care for children, however, are of such special interest to a great many women that they have come to be regarded as "woman's issues." No politician today can afford to ignore these issues. Since the 1970s women have made up the majority of the nation's voters. In the 1984 presidential election, 60.8 percent of eligible women voted, compared with 59 percent of eligible men.

Politicians are responding to this political fact. In his 1980 bid for the presidency, Ronald Reagan vowed to appoint a woman to the Supreme Court after the polls showed his support to be weak among women. Thus, in 1981 Sandra Day O'Connor was named the first woman justice in the 191-year history of the High Court. In the 1984 election, Walter Mondale hoped to gain a political advantage by naming U.S. Representative Geraldıne Ferraro as his running mate. She became the first woman ever to run for Vice-President on a major party's ticket.

One political issue important to women is the passage of the Equal Rights Amendment. The ERA was passed by a two-thirds majority in both

These marchers were part of the new, vocal woman's movement that sprang up in the 1960s and 1970s.

the Senate and the House of Representatives, but it ran into opposition in several states. In 1979, with the deadline for ratification approaching, only three more states were needed to make the ERA the law of the land. Congress extended the ratification deadline to 1982. Much to the disappointment of many American women, however, the ERA failed to win ratification.

The story of the woman's movement in America is not over. Since 1848, it has been a story of spurts of energy and motion followed by little progress for a period of time, and perhaps some backsliding. This continues to be true today. As the twenty-first century approaches, more women hold more jobs at better wages than ever before in history. Yet, men continue to occupy most of the top positions, earning the best salaries, making the final decisions, and still holding the reins of power firmly in their grasp.

Long ago Elizabeth Cady Stanton realized that women had to win the vote. Otherwise, they would never have any say over their own lives or be full citizens of their own country. Elizabeth Stanton was a wise woman. Today, as women continue to struggle for their share in the American dream of "life, liberty, and the pursuit of happiness," women at least have the tool they need. They have the right to vote. And what is more, as Carrie Catt had hoped, they know how to use it.

Despite a victory in both houses of Congress, the ERA failed to win ratification.

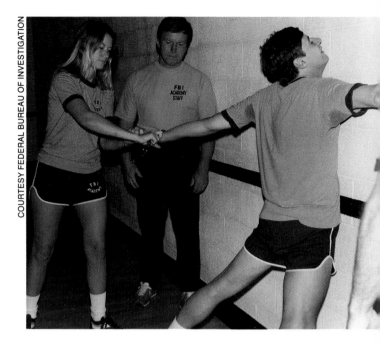

By the 1980s, Women had entered many traditionally male-dominated professions. Here, a woman trains to be an FBI special agent.

F.E.W. SUPPORTS E.R.A.

INDEX

Page numbers in *italics* indicate illustrations

SUGGESTED READING

CONOVER, HUNT, and LINDA GRANT DE PAUW. *"Remember the Ladies."* New York: Viking, 1976.

McHENRY, ROBERT, ed. *Famous American Women.* New York: Dover, 1980.

SMITH, BETSY COVINGTON. The *Breakthrough* series. New York: Walker.

Breakthrough: Women in Religion

Breakthrough: Women in Television

Breakthrough: Women in Law